TRIBAL ECHOES & WHISPERED LOVE

TRIBAL ECHOES & WHISPERED LOVE

Pattye (echo) Thomas

iUniverse, Inc.
New York Lincoln Shanghai

TRIBAL ECHOES & WHISPERED LOVE

All Rights Reserved © 2003 by Pattye Thomas

No part of this book may be reproduced or transmitted in any form or by any means, graphic, electronic, or mechanical, including photocopying, recording, taping, or by any information storage retrieval system, without the written permission of the publisher.

iUniverse, Inc.

For information address:
iUniverse, Inc.
2021 Pine Lake Road, Suite 100
Lincoln, NE 68512
www.iuniverse.com

ISBN: 0-595-28815-4 (pbk)
ISBN: 0-595-74906-2 (cloth)

Printed in the United States of America

I would like to thank so many for their help, in getting my poetry published.
My daughter, Jerrie Solomon, for letting me use her picture on the cover.
Rachel and Jason Sharp for all their help with files.
Melissa Penny for naming my book, Doinan Kavanaugh for all her editing,
And all those that encouraged me to put my poems in a book.

Contents

PART I	TRIBAL ECHOES

POW-WOW	2
A QUIET PLACE	3
CHIEF JOSEPH	4
HIS HEART	5
HUNGRY EYES	5
CHIEF BIG FOOT	6
CHIEF SEATTLE	7
HIS WORDS	8
YOUR VOICE	8
CHIEF SITTING BULL	9
CREATURES OF THE FOREST	10
DEMONS OF THE NIGHT	11
FIRE AND TEARS	12
FIRES OF 2,000	14
FLIGHT	15
FLY FREE	16
FLYING EAGLE	17
GARY SILK	18
GRAY EAGLE	19
HIM	20
WILD AND FREE	20
HOSTAGE HEART	21

LIFE'S LESSONS	22
MARIAS--MASSACRE	23
MEDICINE WHEEL	24
MONTANA	25
MY FRIEND	26
THE MEADOW	27
NIGHT OWL	29
OPPOSITES ATTRACT	30
THE MESSENGER	31
THE QUEST	31
RED DEER	32
SHADES OF GRAY	34
THE DEER TRAIL	34
THE ISLAND	35
THE MOUNTAIN	36
THE MOUSE	37
THE PATH	38
THE TISZA	39
TWILIGHT TIME	40
VANQUISHED	41
WATCHING ME	43
WOUNDED	44
WHITE BUFFALO	45
YOUR VOICE	47
SILVER LIGHT	47

PART II   WHISPERED LOVE

A NIGHT TO REMEMBER	50
A PLACE TO DWELL	51

BLUE WORLD	52
AN APPLE TREE	53
ANGEL	54
BAND OF GOLD	55
CANDLE LIGHT	56
CHALLENGE OF THE MOUNTAIN	57
DAWN	58
DAYLIGHT	59
DON'T CHANGE FOR ME	60
DOUBLE DELIGHT	61
FIRELIGHT	62
FOGGY NIGHT	63
GIVING	64
HELLO LOVE	65
HER TOUCH	66
JUST TO SAY "HELLO"	67
LADDER	68
MORNING MAIL	68
THE LANGUAGE OF LOVE	69
LONGING	71
LOVERS	72
MEMORIES OF YOU	73
MIDNIGHT SUN	74
MIDNIGHT TOUCH	75
MY DREAMS	76
PAINTED ROSE	77
PAINTING	78
THE PALACE	80
PERFECT WORLD	81

POETS AND SINGERS	82
ROSE PETAL	82
SILENT LOVE	83
SILENT SCREAM	84
SLEEPLESS	85
SNOWING	86
SO BOLD	87
STOLEN BLISS	88
SWEET DREAMS	89
THE ARTIST	90
THE LOVE WE SHARE	91
TO AWAKEN YOU	92
TO LIVE A DREAM	93
TRUE LOVE	94
TRUST	95
SKIPPER	95
TWILIGHT TIME	96
TWO YEARS	97
WHISPERS IN THE DARK	98
TRUE LOVE	99
WHEN YOU MAKE LOVE TO ME	100

PART III   MISCELLANEOUS POEMS

MY VALLEY	103
CHAT ROOM CHAT	104
JOHNY ANGEL	105
4 ACES	106
ANDY	107
PARK FRIENDS	108

WIZZARD	109
GUNSLINGER	109
JOKER	110
LOST	111
BULLRIDER	112
COWPOKE	114
"PEAS"	116
STORM	117
COUNTRY GIRL	118
HUGS @ KISSES	119
HAND IN HAND	119
HAPPY TIMES	120
HELL	120
PINK & CRIMSON ROSES	121
"THE DARK"	122

I

Tribal Echoes

POW-WOW

Navaho, Sioux, Cree, Kootenai, and others.
At Pow-Wow they are all like brothers.
To see the dancing, hear the drums,
Don't know the words just hum.
Stick games, black jack, poker too,
There really is a lot to do.
Jingle dancers tinkle as they walk,
Don't want to dance, we'll sit and talk
Teepees pitched-----not in a row,.
Moonlight makes the bead work glow.
Laughing, dancing, or playing games,
The woe in your heart it tames.
Good friends, good food, lots of fun,
Look the evening has just begun!
Grand entry-Chiefs lead the way,
A happy way to spend the day.

A QUIET PLACE

Two small cabins in the mountains
Hid among the towering pines.
It's called a place of quiet
A place to go and clear your mind.

For water there is a spring
Just outside the door.
For light there are the lanterns
Of these there are just four.

There is only a well-hidden road
It's known by only a few.
It is a place for only one,
Yet there are always two.

When I go to the quiet place
One of the braves is sent with me.
He is not there for my company
He may not even talk to me.

The brave is sent for my safety,
I go to meditate you see.
Sweet grass and juniper I burn,
For piece of mind I yearn.

I may stay a week or two.
Time does not matter here,
Thoughts are many, words are few.
The quiet place I hold so dear.

CHIEF JOSEPH

In the cool shadow of an ancient tree
Memories of things long past have come to me.
Wind that blows through swaying pines
Seems to help me write these lines.
I see in my heart a figure on a pony
Silently I watch and smell the scent of sage.
He is here in wisdom and in glory,
As I scratch with pen on empty page.

With eyes that close, I see the Nez Perce
walking 1800 miles, yet 50 miles short their goal.
The dead, the dying the march that took it's toll.
They followed Chief Joseph where he led,
they listened to the words he said.

"The earth is your mother, do not disturb by hoe or plow,
learn to live from what she gives you
all Gods creatures should know how.
Do not move the mountains, or stop a rivers flow,
treat others as you would be treated, this I know.
If you tie a pony do not expect that he will grow,
words matter not, for only deeds do show.
Let things remain, as the Great Spirit made them well
These things I tell my people don't you see?
"Our mother earth is perfect, let it be."
Then quietly he bowed his head and said.
"From where this sun now stands, I shall fight no more forever"
And we shall not forget, THE TRAIL OF TEARS.

HIS HEART

Why do I love him like I do?
Because I know his words are true.
He respects the earth---my mother.
We share the sky-our brother.
Pure water running over stone
Some hear only a babbling brook.
This is the voice of my ancestors!
I love him because he hears
With his heart.

HUNGRY EYES

With hungry eyes I look for you in all the quiet hours,
With empty arms I reach for you, and want you near.
With a lonely heart I dream of you, and longings disappear.
You're close to me, though far away, as one we stay.
Miles and time have no meaning, it slowly fades away.
You're part of me---in each and every way.
You're here with me throughout the longest night.
Here with me in sunshine, or on a cloudy day.
I am yours here for you-in each and every way.

CHIEF BIG FOOT

The Sioux had been defeated, treaties had been signed,
Life as they had known it, forever left behind.
Chief Big Foot old and ill, now with his band at twilight,
Arrived with 300, at Wounded Knee, under the flag of peace.
He could not know what was to happen at daylight,
OH! So slow his journey, wishing the snow would cease.

Their land was lost-----------------they'd no place left to go.
The daylight bugle call rang out, awakening a sleeping tribe.
The skies were angry, unleashing a blizzard-and more Snow.
Shrapnel started shredding lodges,-------------killing all inside.
Uncontrolled insanity,-----------as the troopers shot them down.
The wounded left to die on the cold and frozen ground.

Red Blood now staining the pure white snow.
Butchered lying heaped, and scattered in the dawn.
A helpless tribe with only two rifles they were armed,
Christmas lights and ornaments, were hanging from the rafters,
Only a few wounded upon the straw below could see----------
How all their dreams had ended, at the massacre at Wounded Knee.
Yellow Bird their Medicine Man, So many young, and old,
Because they lost their lives that Morn, this story MUST be told.

CHIEF SEATTLE

A sad wind moans in the distant valley,
and a hush settles over the land;
"Oh! yonder skies weeping your tears,
look down upon my people now so few.
Our warriors have been humbled in defeat.
Now our home land I must sell to you.
The earth is our mother, the sky our brother.

Can you buy the silence of a forest,
a quiet place to listen to a leaf unfurl?
This earth does not belong to man,
but man belongs to earth you see.
How can I sell what I don't own??
NO-this earth does not belong to me!

Mist retreating in the morning sun,
can you sell this; can that be done??
How do you own the sky, or the sparkle
of the tumbling, laughing water??
Man is but a strand of web, not the weaver."

HIS WORDS

His words are sweet and gentle,
And spoken from the heart.
I cherish our times together
I'm sad when we are apart.

He tells me of the moonlight
That shines here in my eyes.
We speak of lighting candles,
This flickering light I idolize.

I know his moods, both good and bad.
He always cheers me when I'm sad.
With a kiss, he starts my day,
Here in his arms I long to stay.

YOUR VOICE

Mesmerizing, tantalizing, loving, caring,
in a way that is all your own.
Your voice like Champagne, so fine,
yet far better then any rare wine.

The opening of a bud from a single rose
our friendship blossomed into love.
No other voice sounds as sweet you see,
as your whisper from Thee--to me.

CHIEF SITTING BULL

Lakota Medicine man and Chief of the Sioux.
How much do you really know about you??
Touring throughout Europe with Buffalo Bill,
Your memory as a leader is with us still.
Your vision at the Sun Dance Ceremony came true.
Custer was defeated, then to Canada you fled.
None came to you hungry and left unfed.
Letting no white man control your footsteps till dead.

The sun rose and set on the land of the Sioux.
Oh! buffalo hunter, counting many coup,
Wise Chief telling your people what to do.
As the earth received the embrace of the sun,
Great Spirit looked down, he knows what you have done.
Last Sioux to surrender, yes that we remember.

When gold was discovered in your sacred land,
You defended the Black Hills with your faithful band.
When you died you were poor, but you died FREE.
Now your words are part of history;
"Each man is good in words in the sight of Great Spirit,
and it is not necessary for Eagles to be crows."
Truth, fable, fantasy or fiction, who really knows??

CREATURES OF THE FOREST

Creatures of the forest are restless, raven cries and streaks across the sky.
Antlered elk paws the ground, whistles then vanishes from sight.
Mamma black bear growls swats at cubs, and sends them up a tree.
Geese quickly leave their quiet pond and take to hurried flight.
Old beaver slaps his tail and dives deep into pond so far below,
Why are all the creatures in the forest restless here tonight?

Mouse runs and hides amidst the wild roses, and its thorns.
Raccoon scurries to find a place within the hollow log.
Soon all the forest creatures will be hidden from sight.
Owl has sent the message, "HIDE for we are not alone".
All is quiet no one moves here in the dark.

Listen! Do you hear them? White mans horses,
Their feet are shod with steel, a jingle of spurs
The breaking of a twig, be silent now and they will pass.
Never knowing the eyes that watch them from afar.
The forest home is safe again, thanks to the owl.

DEMONS OF THE NIGHT

There are moments that take my breath away,
Mornings when I watch the sunrise on a winter day.
See the last brown leaves shake and shiver on the tree!
Now to try and calm the beast inside of me.

We all have dragons, we need to slay.
Hard to keep these beasts at bay.
Oh! here comes the sun in eastern sky,
Warms my soul, keeps spirits high.

There is no place to run no place to hide,
When the demons are there within your mind.
What joy when sunrise chases the darkness away.
The dragons now in hiding as darkness fades away.

FIRE AND TEARS

Scorching heat from noonday sun
Earth parched and dry.
A tinderbox, just waiting to be lit.
<u>THUNDER RUMBLED IN THE SKY!</u>

Hot winds that blew from
South to north.
Absorbing all the moisture that
Was left.
<u>AGAIN THE THUNDER ROARED!</u>

The lightning hit the forest,
Yet not a drop of rain.
Without a moments notice,
The forest was in flame
<u>THE THUNDER CRASHED AGAIN!</u>

Flames leaping dancing high,
From tops of tallest trees.
The heat of sun now nothing
Compared to heat from these.
An inferno! And all within it flee.
<u>THE THUNDER IS NOW SILENT!</u>

The forest is now in ashes
It is there no more.
Fire stopped by gentle tears from
One that cares.
One that wants to save this
Special place for us.
<u>THUNDER A THREAT NO MORE.</u>

The rebirth from the ashes, and
As the Phoenix rose.
Our love will build anew again,
To fly where our hearts chose.

FIRES OF 2,000

Blackened carcasses of deer, elk and bear,
Devastation is everywhere.
Death dots the hillside,
Where once a forest grew.
Eagles circle in the sky,
Above the nests where young did die.
Bewildered doe sheds a tear,
For fawns not fleet enough to flee.

Tall pines like torches blaze,
With fire that lights the sky.
Smoke swirls and settles
In the valley far below.
So thick, day is turned to night.
No rain from father sky,
As mother earth, lies bare.

The lonely cry of the wolf,
Is all that I now hear.
He cries for his mate, and her pups
Dead now in their mountain home.
With paws so burned he can not travel far.
Hot embers singe his shaggy coat,
The sound of pain and despair.
In my dreams that is what I hear.

FLIGHT

Those that fly on wings of lust,
Seldom gain another's trust.
I write in rhyme, that is me
But I am real as can be.

Emotions, thoughts, feelings too
All my words are very true.
They are written for all to see
Rather than a diary.

Words are easy from the heart:
Sad when lovers are apart.
Happy and gay when together,
I even write about the weather.

I let the feelings and words just flow
In what direction I don't know.
Like swallows on a breeze so light,
My mind does wander in the night.

FLY FREE

Oh wounded eagle from the sky,
so glad you saw me passing by.
I'll mend your wounds so you can fly,
once again to soar up high.

Will shelter you from your foes,
give you comfort heaven knows.
I need you well, and watching me.
Rest now!----------then fly free.

Free to watch me from above.
free to tell me of your love.
Healed and rested once again,
I'll set you free to fly again..

For only when your well and free,
you then will return to me.
You will return from far above,
and I will tell you of my love.

FLYING EAGLE

Flying eagle, sometimes solemn and dignified,
Noble elegance and grace, not easily acquired.
Upon his knowledge so many have relied,
By his native people he was so admired.

He had seen the sky weep tears of joy,
To dampen fertile earth so far below.
Holding so much wisdom even as a boy,
So many things this medicine man did know.

The earth is sacred to his people even now.
His spirit walks among them in the mist.
Or on a star lit night, the heavens seem to bow,
As each path he took takes turns and twists.

As a brother to the flowers and the trees,
As a brother to the hills and streams.
One with the eagle, the deer, or a soft breeze,
Still a voice within so many dreams.

Flying Eagle! Hear the murmur of his words in water
Hear his laughter in a sudden clap of thunder.
See him in the clouds so far above.
He is with you one and all-listen! Hear his call?

GARY SILK

A sacred ceremony was done, for even whites to view,
and though you may not understand, I'll tell of this to you.
In protest of the killing of the sacred buffalo,
For long ago the buffalo did give to us his blood.
He fed and clothed us gave us our tools to use.
Today a brave then gave his blood for you.
Gary Silk Lakota Sioux, his flesh was pierced with
wooden sticks, and from here were hung the skulls.
As Silk did dance and smile, his blood began to flow,
tears were shed by many, and their grief did show.
Sticks then torn from his flesh, in honor of the buffalo.
Montana earth did drink the blood and tears,
this ceremony was last done so long ago about
One hundred years.

GRAY EAGLE

Keeping his faith in the Great Spirit above
Gray Eagle set out to steal his love.
Pi-Av young daughter of a great Ute Chief
Promised to another, the promise was brief.

The haunting cry of a lonely dove
the only witness when you took your love.
Gray Eagle, so named for your eyes of blue.
You could of been leader of many.

Now you are remembered by few.
Is love for a woman worth what you gave?
You defied all tradition, so this love was saved!
When night blackened the valley, you slipped away.

Pi-Av (Honey Dew of The Mountain) did go
with her lover Gray Eagle……Out history tells us so,
upon their fast ponies both did ride,
seeking shelter, and a place to hide.

Giving up your role as leader, to follow your dreams.
Beyond tradition, to be with your love, they say.
Pi-Av and Gray Eagle together, now never apart.
Yet banished from their peoples heart.

HIM

It's not the outward him I know,
Nor by his words or his looks.
It's the inner he, I long to see
The love and strength he shares with me.
A part of him, his soul set free.

Looks change! Our bodies
Are but a vessel for our mind.
Tis his inner self I'll find.
That part of him that's deep inside.

WILD AND FREE

I saw an eagle in the sky,
Thought of you as it flew by.
So wild and so free,
It made me think of thee.

No effort to drift on silent wing,
At this sight my heart did sing.
And voices whispered in my mind,
Creator to my friend be kind.

HOSTAGE HEART

I have no right to love you
I knew that long ago.
Knew when we were first together
Just wanted to let you know.

Tried to hide these feelings
That bring so much comfort to me.
Hard to do when head is reeling
Would like for all the world to see.

To see the smile upon my face
To see the laughter in my eyes.
My Love! Will let you, set the pace.
You make me happy do you realize?

So take me in your arms love
It makes my world just right.
As soft and gentle as a dove,
My love is yours tonight.

LIFE'S LESSONS

The hurt is lessening, just a bit each day.
It helped a lot just to go away.
Away from things surrounding me,
That made me think of you.
Thoughts of all the lies and games
You put me through.
I gave to you my heart, bared my soul.
My Trust, my Love was yours to keep.
You knew my love for you was real.
Your words were lies and deceit.
My heart will mend, though scared.
The healing will take time.
I have learned the game you played.
Oh Yes! I learned it well.
You took me to the gates of heaven,
Then dropped me into Hell!
Now I'm free, Free to go my way.
Free to laugh, Free to Love.
Free to live my life each day.
I thank you for this lesson,
'Twas one I shan't forget.
I now know who I am, how I came to be,
Happy am I here with the real me .

MARIAS--MASSACRE

At dawn of light,in the bitter cold
Major Baker, and troops so bold,
Began their slaughter in the snow.
Long past that winter morn on the Marias,
Lonely bluffs in Montana hold a secret well.

But the Marias River has a tale to tell.
Chief Heavy Runner then old and gray,
Under a sign of truce that day.
But scout Cobell--just fired away.
The Springfield's killed 200------
Women, children, and the old.
OH! Yes major Baker was so bold!

You know of Custer and Wounded Knee!
The battle at Marias was hushed up you see.
They lost one trooper…named McKay,
Lying with the dead on that fateful day.
The slaughter began at daybreak and ended
By noon some say, they shot them down,
And then they went away, but the memory
Lives on in Montana History………..

MEDICINE WHEEL

Have you ever wanted to just be alone,
To just sit, and dream and think?
Then come walk with me into the light,
Let the medicine wheel guide you.

When you enter you must face the setting sun.
Now sit quietly, when this is done.
Hear the great Thunder in the west?
Know our ancestors are now at rest.

See the Moon that lights the sky at night?
Give thanks our world was made just right.
Creator gave each bird its song,
And the stars to guide our way.
Along the trail each of us must take.

Not a sound do our moccasins make
A journey in your mind you take.
Notice each tree has its own beauty!
We are the keepers of the land! It is our duty.
God gave us all things, just to use.
Please by greed do not abuse!!

Think with your Heart, and your Head.
Give thanks for each small wonder it is said.
Leave the Wheel, go quietly............
And leave this land like it was meant to be.

MONTANA

What does one say about beauty,
That others have not yet said.
To tell you of my love is my duty,
Don't care what you've heard or read.

Big Sky country it is called by many,
Mountains beyond your wildest dreams.
Of streams, forests, and lakes it has plenty.
Yes the sky is endless, so it seems.

Vast plains to the east, the Rockies divide.
Farming and ranching, hunting there too,
Wheat fields, where pheasant and antelope abide.
But come further west, this I advise you.

Lakes strung about that gleam like pearls,
Ridges, and cliffs, canyons or mountain peaks.
Rivers that tumble, roar, dance and swirl,
Mountain Sheep, Moose, Elk, and Bear of these I speak.

Not only the animals but your heart can roam.
Through canyons, or valleys, or plains, blue sky above.
Yes my love is MONTANA I've made it my home.
Gods answer to a dream, Montana, my love..

MY FRIEND

Tony Mathias died today, I am so sad.
He always had a twinkle in his eyes.
Last Chief of the Kootenai tribe was Tony's dad,
He'd often greet me with a small surprise.

Pow-Wow this year just won't be the same,
Playing sticks all night in his baseball cap.
Tony quietly smiling,----Oh how he loved the game
Sitting there with a woolen blanket on his lap.

His heart was pure, he was so wise,
This medicine man of the Kootenai tribe.
In his quiet way strengthen Nupika ties.
Medicine bag on poles in the corner where
juniper dried.

To outsiders his ways are a riddle,
Most are not welcomed.
Or even care about a culture, they do not understand.
Tony opened a door for me just a little.
Extending his wise but welcomed hand.

Tony Mathias or Madaro, if need be,
Just to have known him, I have been glad,
This old medicine man, with powers unseen.
Now that he's gone, I feel so sad.

THE MEADOW

My mother says I dally,
that I waste time everyday.
I'm up early, do my chores,
then I just slip away.

On happy feet I climb the hill,
and find my friend Old Pine.
Tree with boughs that sweep the ground.
It hides and shelters me.

From here I watch the meadow,
and Oh! what things I see.
Sitting quietly in my secret place.
Beneath this tall old tree.

Just look!! the wind has taken
colors from the rainbow
and dumped them far below.
Tiny flowers midst the green.

A fawn wobbles and stands,
Old doe paws and stomps her feet.
She worries so.
I think she's saying.
"Come hurry son, lets go."

Red tailed hawk circles in the sky,
He's watching for movement far below.
Darn!! I missed them, doe and fawn
Have vanished in the forest.

Oh, there is a bear with cubs,
Blue black raven begins to call.
Soft breezes send the meadow dancing.
Raven's shadow passes by.

Now I must leave the meadow.
A place I know so well.
T'was here I learned of birth, life and death.
My class room, what tales the meadow tells.

NIGHT OWL

Night owl in the midnight sky,
Above the moonlit valley: Oh so high.
Wise owl that never sleeps at night
With out spread wings you're quite a sight

Quiet power, hidden strength, yet grace,
By the light of dawn there will be no trace
Of the hunter or the hunted in the dark.
Wings, enfold your prey, talons leave a trace.

A trace of night owl, no one ever sees,
As no one watches the hunter of the night.
Just a whisper on a moonlit breeze.
A conquest ended by your silent flight.

OPPOSITES ATTRACT

When we were young, we did not know,
The kind of boys we liked.
But all of us knew the type we didn't.
A friend said, "no long haired, uneducated, messed-up vet."
And above all else, not white.
She met a man he was all of the above,
They fell in love one night.

Yes opposites attract
The cold of ice-----The heat of fire.
Your tender love-----My fierce desire.
Hardness of steel-----Softness of thistle.
Your loud clear voice-----My gentle whistle.
Whiteness of snow-----Blackness of night.
Your boisterous way-----My rapt delight.
Sweetness of honey-----Taste of a lime.
Your sense of reality-----My love sublime.
Tall rugged mountain-----Low peaceful valley.
Your sense of urgency-----My tend to dally.
The swiftness of light-----The pace of a snail.
My skin so brown-----And yours so pale.

THE MESSENGER

The call of the owl does not echo,
Yet his message is loud and clear.
Taking his words to those that need to hear.
Watching on the plains, and in the forest.

Silent and hidden in the light of day.
Swift and sure on powerful wings,
Deer in the forest, pause and lift their heads
Listening quietly to what the wise owl says.

The hoot of the owl does not echo.
Have you ever wondered why?
Stop and listen to his message,
As he sails across the sky.

THE QUEST

Can we eliminate the demons in our minds?
Forget the past, leave it behind?
Erase the wrongs make things right,
Will we find restful sleep at night?
Will we look to the future without fear?
Is there someone out there that will hear?
Is their hope, beyond despair?
Can we find peace, is it there?
Take my hand show me the way.
I am lost, confused what can I say?
These are questions I ask myself.
I know it is darkest, before the dawn.

RED DEER

In the sun drenched valley midst the pines
A shot rang out from far above.
A single rifle shot that took my love.
Red Deer lying hurt and dying,
Yet with a smile upon her lips.
I held her to me tightly as she touched my fingertips;

"Lone Eagle take no revenge, just hold me close
To you, for blood gets blood and pain brings pain
Yes this I know is true.
Our people need you---you are the leader of our tribe.
Please hold me and hear the words I say!

I will not see the sun set at the end of day,
We've ridden many miles together to hunt the buffalo
We've seen many winters and the snow.
I've borne your sons now hold me as I die.
Do not let our people see you if you cry.

Give my new moccasins to Silver Swan,
For hers are old and worn.
Take my buckskin dress to Feather
As hers is badly torn.
My faithful pony is for Robin, dear friend of mine.
Tell him treat her kindly, a swifter mount he will not find.

Lay me to rest in our hidden place upon the hill.
Take me there when all is quiet and still.
OH! I feel your lips upon my eyes now closed.
Hold no malice in your heart of things now past.
Remember as the sun does rise my spirit will go free.
No pain, No hunger, No worldly thing will bother me.

Lone Eagle you have loved me well, now I must rest."
Red Deer is at our special place that only few do know.
But her vision is here with me, every where I go.

SHADES OF GRAY

My world is shades of gray outside the door.
The smell of blossoms on morning air.
My lovers voice I softly hear.
Rays of sunlight will soon light the sky.

The birds will sing, the night will die.
We stand together, here just at dawn.
I watch a mountain blue bird as it takes flight.
Soon sun will rise and steal the night.

Like the heart my lover stole from me.
He keeps it there with him you see.
He guards it well, I'm safe and free,
Because he holds that small part of me.

THE DEER TRAIL

Today I took a walk on the trail of the deer.
I followed it from mountain side to valley floor.
Through hidden meadows, I'd not seen before.
Warmth from sun making dapples on the land.
Shadows danced, as tall pines swayed.
Cool clear stream, chattered as it flowed.
The voices in the forest beckoned me,
I knew I was not alone, birds twittered
A butterfly flew by. The hoot of an owl I heard.
Oh the voices of the forest made my heart sing.
On the trail of the deer, I was not alone.

THE ISLAND

There is an island surrounded by water so blue,
Jagged cliffs, tall pines, mountain sheep and deer there too.
An island not so very far from shore,
Quiet waters in the bay, Oh! Who could ask for more?

Lonely mystic lovely island, not a soul in sight
Short visit to this tiny place brings such delight.
On the island with a friend, whispering seems right
Dreaming dreams, sharing thoughts, makes a heart so light.

Beautiful by moonlight, water looks like jewels,
Glittering and gleaming in the shadow of the moon.
Here in this secluded spot nature makes the rules.
Soft breezes in the pines just hum a tune.

Small island where one can go to dream,
Listen in the darkness for a familiar sound!
Watch the twinkle of a star, look upon a moonbeam
Idle thoughts, happy memories, tranquility abounds.

Magnificent at dawn when the day is new,
Listen to the birds sing, this I share with you.
Watch a new born fawn, or see an eagle dive,
On this island you will know the joy to be alive.

THE MOUNTAIN

Take me to that special place, far above the valley floor.
Hold my hand and call me Darling like before.
Listen to the rustle of the leaves,
Watch the swaying of the trees!
Feel the raindrops gently falling,
Listen to the Spirits, Calling, Calling.

Water cold and sparkling from a stream,
Houses look so tiny so far below
OH! What a quiet place to dream!!
My love my thoughts are with you, you know.
Do you recall the echoes of our laughter??

Peace and joy that was ours to share,
Together on a mountain top so far away.
Memories here in my heart, here to stay.
I dream of returning there someday.
On the mountaintop, call me Darling like before.

THE MOUSE

A small gray mouse in the meadow played,
Basking in the sunshine, resting in the shade.
Though danger lurked at each and every bend,
Mouse romped and played, no fear within.

The coyotes, wolves, and creatures of prey
well they eyed her so hungrily that day.
Mouse had no fear, she stopped to rest
she knew her friends were the best.

An Eagle had fallen out of the sky,
hurt and wounded, he could not fly.
Mouse called the Owl, her friend of old,
The wise Owl fed the Eagle so bold.

Small gray mouse in the meadow plays.
The Eagle watches her through the days.
Small gray mouse, dancing in the moonlight
safe in the shadow of the Owl at night.

THE PATH

As down the path of life I wander
Stop to rest, and mind doth ponder
This journey we all must make,
What turn is right, which a mistake.

I have not always walked or chosen,
The road ahead so broad and wide
Rather did I often take a hidden trail
An easy place to go and hide.

A path so hidden in shadows,
A place where few would go
Why I chose that lonely trail
So few will ever know.

But choose I did, it is behind me,
Now I walk here in the light.
Shadows of the past receding,
Only moonlight, here tonight.

THE TISZA

And the river spread death throughout the land,
Poisoned by greed for gold, the greed of man.
Clouds wept for the loss, shed tears from above,
Soft breezes whispered their words of love.

People need to be taught to take care of their home,
Water teaming with fish, lands where the animals roam.
Vast forests, and oceans, mountains and valleys,
Ours to cherish and care for not to waste by folly.

May hearts awaken, know the wrong that they do,
"Great Spirit help them," I ask this of you.
The Tisza now haunted by ghosts of the past,
How long will this destruction last?

TWILIGHT TIME

As shadows lengthen outside my door,
evening sun sinks in the west,
visions appear, and voices on a breeze
sounds muffled by the swaying trees.

Shadows dance, dim the day
soon darkness will be here to stay.
At just that special moment at night,
part dusk, part dark, yet part light.

My mind then wanders for a spell
and of the past my thoughts do dwell.
The visions come, they talk to me!
Oh how great if all could see.

See the shadows from the past
hear the voices of long ago.
How I wish this time could last
voices tell me things I need to know.

A paradox of dark and light
soft gray shadows that come at night,
bringing the voices and visions I see,
like ghostly Spirits watching over me.

VANQUISHED

Somewhere in the smoke of our fire
the truth of yesterday you will see.
Then you will know of the rage in me.

Your children had smallpox,
you wrapped them in robes.
These were then given to us
as we had no clothes.
We died like the buffalo,
like the forests you took.
Your destruction killed
all the fish in the brook.

You slaughtered the buffalo their
bones now bleached white as snow.
You ran off the wild animals
OH! Where did they go??

"Anger! Frustration! Starvation!"
These things do not make a good combination.
We ate our dogs, and our horses too.
These things you forced us to do.

We lived for generations off the land,
and left it the way that it was.
Not for greed or for profit……
as the white man does………………………….

Starvation was common, nowhere to go,
we prayed to the gods for the buffalo.
They fed us clothed us, sheltered us too.
Without the buffalo, what can we do??

The young and the old were first to die
mothers held babies too weak to cry.
Now our way of life is gone forever.
But our beliefs will never waver..

WATCHING ME

With a watchful eye he turns his head
Does he know I am in bed??
With wings outspread he glides up high.
Does he hear my wistful sigh??
With power and grace he quietly flies
Does he know I watch the sky??

He sees me and he tips a wing,
Does he know what daylight will bring??
As darkness slowly turns to dawn
Does he know my fears are gone??
Oh great Eagle, So wild, So free
I'm glad your watching over me.

WOUNDED

Like a wounded animal, that in the forest abides,
My first instinct was to run away and hide.

To hide from the hunter that caused my pain.
To rebuild the energy, that love has drained.

To heal my lonely shattered heart
To learn to live alone……apart.

Now another tells me of his love,
Was he sent from far above?

In his arms can I trust again?
Does his love come from within?

From deep within his inner soul,
Is to comfort, love and protect his goal?

Hold me close my love if you care,
My thoughts with you I want to share.

WHITE BUFFALO

So many, many moons ago, in sacred hills of Dakota
Appeared a beautiful Indian girl, seen by two Lakota.
One Lakota brave looked at her with only lust,
The other gazed, he saw her beauty, gained her trust.

"Step forward", said this vision of such beauty
"You must listen to my word that is your duty."
One warrior ran to her with impure thoughts
His heart was turned to stone, the flesh stripped from his bones.

The other warrior kneeled, he was now alone.
No lust within his heart, for which he must atone.
He knelt there before her in bewilderment.
None other like her had he seen or met.

A white buffalo calf now appeared before his eyes,
Then it changed again--into a lady in the sunrise.
She was now holding a bundle in her hand.
Speaking softly she now said, "I will walk now in your land.

Seven sacred ceremonies you must learn to do."
They followed her instructions, knew her words were true.
The sweat lodge, the naming, the healing, the adoption,
The marriage, the sundance. The seventh--The vision quest
That will be revealing.

The people listened; they learned these lessons well.
For generations, this tale they would tell.
When the white buffalo returns again, And it will
There will be peace and harmony anger will be stilled.

The earth our mother, cannot be inherited by others.
We are just to be its keeper, all like brothers.
Borrowing this land and keeping it safe you see,
For generations yet unborn! Oh let this vision be.

YOUR VOICE

Mesmerizing, tantalizing, loving, caring,
in a way that is all our own.
Your voice like champagne, so fine,
yet far better the any rare wine.

The opening of a rose from a single bud
our friendship blossomed into love.
No other voice sounds as sweet you see,
as your whisper from thee to me.

SILVER LIGHT

The rainbows colors, what a sight!
Setting sun in all its glory,
Yet none compares to moons soft light.
Oh to watch those silver rays,
Light up my lover's eyes
No sunrise or sunset I've seen
Equals the splendor of that silver light.

II

WHISPERED LOVE

A NIGHT TO REMEMBER

Sweet smell of mother earth, scent of
Freshly mown hay.
Stars twinkle so high above,
Sent here to light our way.
Beneath a moonbeam, hand in hand
Contented now with you I stand.

No longer dreaming, but here with you,
Seeing with my eyes and not my mind.
Touching with fingertips, as I have longed to do,
Beyond imagination, leaving dreams behind.
At the reality of your caress I tremble,
Knowing now my dream came true.

I find no words so I just hold you,
Close beside you, not knowing what to do.
I feel your heartbeat next to mine.
Passion and love are again reborn.
Together in a closeness dreams do not compare,
No words needed to let you know I care.

A PLACE TO DWELL

Your body is only a place for your soul to dwell.
It is your mind, your heart, I love so well.
Your gentle touch., your soft caress,
Those are what I love the best.
Your loving arms that hold me tight.
Your voice here in my ear at night.

So these are the reasons I love you.
The contentment, when I am by your side.
Sparkling laughter, things we share.
I want you happy--as happy as you make me.
You bring wonderment and joy to me.
To feel safe when I am close to you.
These are some of the reasons I love you.

BLUE WORLD

Today the color of my world is BLUE;
Thoughts on my mind are all of you.
Wanting just to hold you close to me,
To shelter you from harm you see.

You found your way into my heart,
No my LOVE, we will not part.
You're here with me inside my soul,
To care for you is now my goal.

BLUE days, BLUE nights, no tender sighs,
My love look deeply into my eyes!!!
Please know my love is just for you,
Without your love, my world is BLUE

AN APPLE TREE

Our love is like the growing of a simple apple tree.
From just a seed to ripened fruit,
That's how it came to be.
It started with a little seed, then a twig did sprout.

With barren branches reaching upwards to the sun,
And buds that burst to bloom in spring
Then with fully opened blossoms, scent that lingers
And nighttime can't erase, like the blush of love

There upon your face.
As petals fall in days of summer sun and lie there
Softly on the ground.
The tiny fruit comes forth, to grow and swell

In days so long and warm.
To ripen has our love has, with passing
Of the time, a rosy glow that only
Fruitful love does know.

ANGEL

I felt an angel's touch last night
A dream maker to make my dreams just right.
Nightmares are gone, just chased away
Awakened and ready to greet the day.

An angel was sent from so far above
Bringing the gift of a special love.
Love not built on passion or desire
Caring, liking, sharing, a love to acquire.

An angel and so soft was the touch
But OH! a touch that meant so much.
A vision that reached me in the night
A feeling and it made my day so bright.

It made me look beyond the obvious to see
And realize that others care for me.
The wind made music outside my door
And my restless nights are here no more.

BAND OF GOLD

It hurts to see the longing in her eyes,
it breaks my heart at night because she cries.
I know I can not love her as I should
with all my heart I wish I could.
She cares for me with such tenderness,
but I know there is a smoldering fire inside.
Should let her go, just set her free I guess,
the longing in her eyes she tries to hide.
I am so content just to have her near,
yet to her it is not fair.
OH! it hurts to hear her cry!
knowing my pain she shares.
Must I leave her to show how much I care
and take away the band of gold,
that keeps her here??

CANDLE LIGHT

The flickering of one lone candle
casts shadows on your skin.
Your lips, your hands, your touch
taking me where I have never been.

To pleasures heights; Oh so high,
beyond the stars up in the sky.
Pleasures of the body and the soul,
my world now in your control.

Like fireworks, on the 4th of July,
or defining thunder in the sky.
My love, what pure delight
you bring to me by candlelight.

CHALLENGE OF THE MOUNTAIN

He looks in awe-struck silence
At the beauty OH!-------so high,
This rocky craggy mountain
That reaches to the sky.

It stands there in the dawn
Unchallenged yet this day
The clouds are like a halo
That the sun will burn away.

I watch him from so far below
In the early morning light
He will scale that mountain in the distance,
And return to me at night.

So I patiently await the sunset
I wait in hope,------not in fear
For when the sun is setting
I know my love will soon be here.

The challenge of the mighty mountain
It is there!!----So he will climb
As the shadows lengthen in the valley
I know his love will soon be mine.

DAWN

Fear not the hours before the dawn
Soon its velvet softness will be light.
In the darkest hours, think of me
Know I am watching you tonight.

Hear my voice upon the breeze
Whispering to calm your mind.
Know I am near you in the dark
Rest well leave troubles behind.

Think of only sun filled days!
Listen to the joy of laughter.
Happiness of greeting a new dawn.
Shadows now will soon be gone.

DAYLIGHT

My hand transgresses across my bed,
To touch the pillow where you lay your head
I inhale and smell the scent of you.
Thoughts of last night are coming through.

Thoughts of when you were close to me,
Precious moments that were meant to be .
My mind knows not if daylight is near,
With eyes still closed I linger here.

Yes here in happy contented bliss
Remembering your soft sweet kiss.
Here in memories and dreams of you,
Knowing this love was shared by two.

DON'T CHANGE FOR ME

I loved you when you flew free,
will not clip your wings to be with thee..
Do not want to erase your identity
want you to be you, me to be me.

I love you just as you are now.
I could not change, would not know how.
Your mind, your heart, and your soul you see.
these are the things that matter to me.

Our love and passion, calms the night
turning ghosts and shadows into light.
The truth is not buried in a grave of lies,
I found acceptance in your kind eyes.

We are very different, yet alike somehow.
So do not change, stay as you are now.
Together my love we'll find the way
To stay just as we are this day.

DOUBLE DELIGHT

There is a beautiful rose named Double Delight.
The petals a mixture of red and off white.

Oh; that name what it brings to my mind,
To try and write, words are so hard to find.

Like a witch with a kettle mixing a brew,
My mind conjures up an image of two.

Two friends together, alone in the dark,
Hand in hand, for a walk in the park.

Double Delight!!, when these words I see,
I think of a lover alone here with me.

Double!-Like two---us together, me and you.
Delight!-bring pleasure, this we can do.

With soft caresses, and a tender touch,
Giving pleasure can mean so much.

Pleasure for both is Double Delight.
Two lovers together, sharing the night.

FIRELIGHT

Flames from the burning fireplace
Cast fleeting shadows on your face.
I touch you with my fingertips
Then kiss you gently on the lips.

Soft snow is falling from above
So cozy to cuddle with my love.
A little wine, the music is so low
Playing our song, the words we know.

Contented here in this quiet place,
Far from the city, it's crowds, the race.
Strong winds sway the pines tonight,
Inside it's warm, and all is right.

Dreaming dreams, and sighing sighs,
Gazing into your kind blue eyes.
My lover's arms, holding me
There is no place I would rather be.

FOGGY NIGHT

Was in the fog with my love so near
he held me close, whispering in my ear.
His arms around me felt so right,
The fog grew thicker in the night.

As gentle hands caressed my breast,
I lay my head upon his chest.
His lips are now so close to mine,
Oh! This feeling is so sublime.

My lovers desire excites me so,
breathing quickens as passions grow.
The fog envelopes us in our delight,
lovers together, on a foggy night.

GIVING

To put your body, between mine
and the stars.
To know this night
is forever ours.
To totally give myself,
freely this I do.
Patiently lead and guide me,
this I ask of you.
With velvet softness-----
hold me close.
Gaze into my eyes, I'm frightened
don't you realize??
Quietly whisper "I love you",
even if you lie.
Feel my body tremble at your touch.
Not gold or riches do I have,
myself I offer you.
I give the only thing I have.
My love----------for you.

HELLO LOVE

I took the words you said one time,
And then I put them in a rhyme.
These are your words, that is true,
Now I'll send them back to you.

I see the starlight in your eyes,
Put there by love, I realize.
You are so very----very near
Here in my heart, you're with me dear.

Just as sunrise starts each new day,
Then sunset kisses that day away.
We gaze upward at stars above.
Thinking together of the one we love.

Each tiny star up in the sky,
Was put there just for you and I.
They twinkle and say, "Hello my Love."
A message in the sky, so far above.

Between us there is never a goodbye,
Only later Love of mine.
When it is time to be at rest,
That is the time I like the best.
Here so close my dear to you,
In evening shadows, or morning dew.
With you here always, in my heart,
Stars say, "Hello" when we are apart.

HER TOUCH

I feel her reach for me at night,
So sleep I fain to longer enjoy
That gentle loving touch .
Her nails so softly on my skin
A sigh escapes my lips,
Then I turn to her and
Now the caressing will began.

My lips upon her breasts so light,
Soft sweet kisses in the night.
Words to whisper in her ear,
Words to tell her that I care.
Her arms encircle me with love.
Her eyes lit by moonlight from above.

My breathing quickens, as passions rise
From my love, just soft sweet sighs.
Her hands now draw me close to her,
My muscles tense, we are so close.
I feel my love from head to toe.
Wrapped in my arms, here with me
Soon to be one is our destiny.

JUST TO SAY "HELLO"

In my northern world fresh from hibernation
There now descends the blush of spring.
Tiny wild flowers are dancing in the breeze
As summer sun is showing golden
In the early hours of mystic morn.

Hearing your voice, tender, soothing and
Gentle, so sublime it took my breath away.
Oh my love how wonderful to call you
Just to say, "HELLO" as you start the day.
Your soft voice asking, "How are you?"

Speaking words in rhyme to say, "I love you too."
Lilies in a field of clover, seem to gently sway,
keeping time as I spoke to you-------today.
I am saving this moment in my memory.

LADDER

Building a ladder to reach the stars,
The ladder is love the love is ours.
Building it slowly rung by rung,
So I can climb when it is done.

Building with trust and desire.
Watching it grow higher and higher.
Building it strong it is made for two.
Waiting to climb this ladder with you.

MORNING MAIL

Crumpled up the pages, of the words you sent to me;
They were so personal, for only my eyes to see.
As a whisp of smoke rose, curling in the air,
I cried a quiet cry, and thought this isn't fair.
No need to cry, no need for tears, you see
They are not lost, but forever stored in memory.
Sweet---sweet words, that you wrote to me.

THE LANGUAGE OF LOVE

(His words to her)
Speaking to her in a language not her own,
she answers with her teeth upon my shoulder.
Her nails write lines of love, across my back.
The way is steep and wonderful to go
a little risky, but worth each step I take.
With tongue following each soft fold and crevice
I find and taste the hidden spots
that she has never known.
Her gentle trembling does tell me
I am her one and only love
and we are speaking in a language all our own.

(Her words to him)
As I write my words of love
upon your back,
I do so--so very tenderly.
My eyes will close, my heart will sing.
As you make love to me.
Your words quite often, I don't know,
but with your touch, you speak to me.
My trembling is not in fear,
my sigh is that of lust.
My body and my mind is in your trust.
With gentle hands do hold me,
with gentle words do speak.
The words of love are there and
in what language I don't care.

We speak with bodies, minds and souls.
The language of LOVE.

LONGING

Longing to feel two hearts
Beat as one.
Longing to rest at night
When day is done.
Longing to feel your touch
Upon my skin.
Longing to know the warmth
Of passion again.
Longing to give my trust
To another.
Longing to love again as
I have loved no other.

LOVERS

Butterflies that flutter in the sun,
A soft caress, when day is done.
Gentle breeze that blows at night
In your arms all seems right.
Misty morn, flowers wet with dew,
All these things remind me of you.

The flame of a candle, a glass of wine,
So many things do come to mind.
Little love notes you wrote to me.
Eyes that sparkle, I long to see.
Your tenderness, your loving smile,
Just hold me darling for a while.
Thinking of you writing simple lines
And dreaming dreams of other times.
We share the same sky up above.

MEMORIES OF YOU

As the moon climbs higher in the sky,
Thoughts of you go drifting by
Other times, other places, far away
I wonder how you spend each day.
I imagine that I can see your smile,
Or walk with you for just a while.

Is parting worth the pain?
Yes and I would do it all again.
Time not lost but there with you,
In spirit and in body too.
In sweet embrace I cling to thee,
Building-----memories you see!!.

So far apart, and yet------so near,
Your voice at night I long to hear.
Soft music playing in the dark,
Voices laughing in the park.
All these things are here with me,
In my treasure chest of memories!!
OH!! SWEET MEMORIES..

MIDNIGHT SUN

I hear his voice and the world fades away,
Turning my darkest hour into a sunlit day
Does he hear the longing in my sigh,
As he kissed away a teardrop in my eye?

We dream together at light of day
The shadow of the moon then fades away.
We come together, we are now as one
In a surreal world of the midnight sun.

Full moon drifting in the eastern sky.
Blood red it shines up there so high.
Not a star can I see this night
Oh no there is nary a one in sight.

Red moon watches from up above
Bringing thoughts of my love.
Does he watch the moon same as I
And think of me at it shines up high??

MIDNIGHT TOUCH

As I feel your hands upon my skin,
It makes me want to love again.
Slowly warming to your touch,
Your gentle touch that means so much.

Love, listen to my soft sighs
As I close my gray green eyes.
Listen to my heartbeat, when you hold me tight.
Your lips upon my eyelids in the night.

There is no need for words now
As passions build within.
Your tongue is now touching me,
Where your fingertips have been.

Is this a dream my Loved one,
Bringing me such delight?
If so I want to stay asleep
And dream this dream all night.

Your soothing voice, next to my ear.
You're saying all the things I want to hear
Two lovers together as one,
Contented now when day is done..

MY DREAMS

In early morn, before the dawn
When sun has yet to light the sky,
I waken with thoughts of one
I have not met, yet hold so high.

It is comforting knowing she is here
In thoughts and dreams so near.
Memories and tender words to treasure,
Thoughts of her that give me pleasure.

I see the silhouetted trees
Against the silent stars,
And dream of a time that sight
Will be just ours.

Her voice in my mind I hear
Her face a vision but oh so clear.
I know her by faith you see
My love is here in dreams with me.

PAINTED ROSE

What is it that guides an artist's brush,
Turning negative space, to a meadow lush?
Or painting mountains white with snow,
What is it…I really would like to know?
What force, what power guides the hand that
Captures the beauty of our land?

To create the one, the perfect rose.
OH! cannot be done by poets and pros
A rose of beauty that never dies
Remains forever, before our eyes.
Take for me what guides your hand
And paint the rose, for which I stand.

My symbol of all that I love so dear,
A rose so I may have it here.
It's everlasting beauty here with me,
Please paint one rose for me!!

PAINTING

Painting this picture just for you,
Any place we are together will do.
Soft breezes, moonlight, candles dimly glow,
All is quiet, but the calling of a crow.

So peaceful in my cabin in the pines,
Our lips can meet and arms entwine.
You're home at last, true love of mine.
No need to talk, there is no time.

Just hold me in the fading light,
Your closeness turns a wrong to right.
To wake together as dawn is near.
I'm painting this picture for you my dear.

A picture of quiet joy and content.
Memories to last throughout the day.
Of happy hours, so joyously spent.
A picture in your mind, when you're away.

Lingering scent of perfume in the air,
Visions of unbraiding my long dark hair.
Memories of a soft voice in the night,
Hope you find this picture just right.

When days are so busy, so much to do,
Just remember this picture I painted for you.
A painting of a quiet moonlit night,
So then your world will be right.

To paint with words is what I do,
So I am painting thoughts for you.
To ease your lonely troubled heart,
And see with your mind when we are apart.

THE PALACE

Standing in the courtyard, looking at the stars
Waiting for the break of day, now not far away.
Each thinking of a love that is theirs,
Each hoping they will meet when they pass this way.

Walking midst a moonbeam, heart a flutter,
Two ladies each are waiting for their lover.
Lovers now gone and they do not know where.
For their safe return is all they now do care.

Oh the nights are lonely when you are alone.
Caesar has sent their loves to conquer Rome.
Two ladies, both so alone, one with raven hair
Two ladies, that have so much to share.

A gentle lady with hair like suns first light.
Hoping her love is safe this night.
Listening to the footsteps of the guards,
Oh just to wait not knowing is so hard.

Have they fallen in battle, are they well?
At daylight the scout will have news to tell.
Oh the sun is rising, soon both will know
If their loves are safe, then and only then,
Caesar's ladies will go, but only when they know.

PERFECT WORLD

If I were to make a perfect world, would have
to create high mountains to stand guard
Above my quiet valley, wild flowers ever blooming in the yard.
Small stream rambling through a meadow would be grand.
For you a lofty mountain, for me a meadow,
this perfect world I have planned.

You can climb the mountain! I would not dare.
May your journey so long and tiring fulfill your soul.
I know your heart is on the mountain, please take care!
Waiting for you in the valley is my goal.

Soft low music, fireplace is burning fine
A few dim candles omit a pleasant glow.
To have you with me in the night is so divine,
I miss you when you are on the mountain, you know.

You will go again tomorrow, climbing suits you well.
Again I wait in my peaceful valley for the night,
Your return is what I live for, my thoughts on you do dwell.
When you are in my arms again, my world will be right.
I will see the mountain through your eyes.
Ich kann die Berge Durch deine Augen sehen.)

POETS AND SINGERS

We've played and laughed, talked all day,
And now we'll love the night away.
And poets would write, and singers would sing
If they were to know what pleasure we'd bring.

Two lovers together under moonbeams and stars,
Both knowing this night was ours, just ours.
You'd reach for me, I'd be close to you,
We would kiss and caress, as two lovers do.

And poets would write, and singers would sing
If they were to know what pleasure we'd bring.
When kissing and caressing, finally was done
Two lovers together, would then become one.

ROSE PETAL

He picked up a fallen petal
From the rose beside my bed.
Then gently wiped away the tear
I could not help but shed.
Leaning closer to me
He whispered in my ear,
"Your tears of joy excite me Love."
Oh!! What sweet words to hear.

SILENT LOVE

Standing at my window in the starlight,
Waiting for the start of day.
Slightly shivering in the dark of night
My love stands behind me, not a word to say.

Together we love to watch the rising sun,
Knowing we will be together when day is done.
Strong arms encircle me and draw me near.
Yet not a whisper do I hear.

I feel his breath upon my cheek,
I turn to him and tongue does seek
The taste and the texture of his skin.
Yet not a word does come from him.

My breath quickens as passions rise.
No longer do we watch the skies.
I stand now in my Loves embrace.
Soft kisses, soft sighs leave no trace.

The silk gown warms against my skin,
Where my lovers hands have been.
His lips upon my body leave me weak,
Yet no words do we speak

Bright morning sun, dawn is here,
All is well my Love is here.
Here to hold me in the night,
Here to start the day just right.

SILENT SCREAM

Undoing the buttons on your shirt
Opening them slowly—one—by--one.
My tongue trails kisses down your chest,
With arms encircling, I draw you to by breast.

I hear your rapid breathing! Oh so clear.
Two hearts beating together, now my dear.
Your skin is warm upon my lips,
Now to touch with just my fingertips.

To see the moonlight in your eyes
And listen to your heartfelt sighs.
Just being in your arms---what glee,
What joy, what ecstasy, you bring to me.

Emotions flowing, wild as a mountain stream,
You hear my voice--in a silent scream.
Just now!! This moment!! No future!! No past.
Only loving memories of you will last.

SLEEPLESS

My loves desire was stilled too soon,
Yet he still looks to me for love.
I listen to soft music and hum a tune,
The voice I hear is gentle as a dove.

I can not live in memories of the past.
There's lots of fun and laughter in the daytime.
Sometimes I wish the day would ever last.
Nighttime, nightmares, sleepless nights are mine.

Do not want to see what the future holds,
Hard to look longingly to my life ahead.
If I could ask my god, but am not that bold,
Not the future, or the past, it's night I dread.

When sleeping all alone dreams stop by.
Try and crowd them out, stay awake if I can.
It's then I think of long ago and sometimes cry,
Dreams are not fun when you know the end.

Daytime is fine I've lots of work to do,
Nights I hate, most are hard to get through.
Can't escape responsibilities, they keep me home.
Just hate to go to bed when I'm alone.

SNOWING

Yesterday was long and cold
I sat here and I watched it snow.
Flakes dancing in the winter air
As I write lines that say I care.

All is white the world is still,
My fire is cozy, my heart will fill
With words of your love
As pure as snowflakes from above.

The snow has turned my world white,
I write these words by candlelight.
Tomorrow when the dawn is near
I know my love will soon be here.

SO BOLD

Oh my love I've been so bold,
Telling you my dreams as they unfold.
And how I think of you each day
And dream to pass the time away.

Dreams that bring you close to me.
As close as if you're here you see.
Dreams of being in your arms,
Dreams that set off fire alarms.

Dreams of a raging passion, a desire
Dreams that set my soul on fire.
Yet I wonder when we meet,
Will our love be as sweet?

As sweet as dreams oh, what a joy.
So I dream, when we are apart.
Then my love when I'm with you.
I know that all my dreams are true.

We will love and be so bold,
Telling things we've left untold.
Doing things we want to do.
Dreams come true my love with you.

STOLEN BLISS

I long for a time of stolen bliss
As passions awaken from your kiss.
To feel your body tremble as you hold me,
The desire in your eyes I want to see.

To hear your breathing quicken in the dark
As flames ignite from just a spark.
Dreaming of your hands upon my skin,
Caressing, arousing, as I have never been.

To feel the tingling in my breasts
Lying with my head upon your chest.
When your lips trail kisses down my spine
Oh!! My love that is sublime.

As you place your hands beneath my hips,
I'll kiss you softly on the lips.
Whispering as my tongue finds your ear.
Hoping to tell you what you want to hear.

So when my darling there are no words to say,
I know you will take my fears away.
With gentle passion love me your way,
Making memories to last throughout the day.

The scent, the feel, the taste of my love,
With my body below, and yours above.
Could this thought be wrong, yet feel right?
My darling I long for you at night.

SWEET DREAMS

From the castles of your land,
To the vast plains of mine.
Words flow freely from us both
For we live within our minds.

So vastly different, yet much the same,
Within our hearts a fire burns
Words to each other calm the flame.
The longings for which we yearn.

OH! To just close my eyes and see
The flickering firelight in your eyes.
To know your heart belongs to me,
As I remember the moonlit skies.

Our thoughts travel across the miles
Thoughts and memories that make us smile.
Sweet dreams to get us through the night,
Anticipation of a love so right.

THE ARTIST

The artist with his pallet and paint,
Transferring images from mind with brush.
The poet, neither sinner or saint,
Words sometimes tangle in the rush.

Just a little ink upon an empty page,
Little ink that causes, laughter, love or rage.
A little paint, when brush strokes are right
Portray a shadow, or cast a light.

Colors, shades, shapes, tint and hue,
To mix and blend, is what he'll do.
The poet writes, and dreams so true,
Words pour forth, here to you.

The artist not always happy with his work.
The poet sometimes sounds like a jerk.
Yet part of each, is in what they do.
My dear, I love each part of you.

So please paint something just for me.
It's the inner you I long to see.
Have tolerance when you read my lines,
I hope an inner beauty you will find.

THE LOVE WE SHARE

I need to feel your arms around me tight
Your body close to mine tonight.
To touch you gently in the dark,
And watch as flames grow from a spark.

Oh! Your breath upon my cheek
This feeling as my knees go weak.
Your loving touch upon my skin
And then the kisses will begin.

To kiss you on the neck and whisper
In your ear, "Tonight I need you dear."
I need your love to feel complete,
I need to hear your voice so sweet.

I need to feel the rapture, and the love,
My body below, yours above.
Between me and the outside world
You see, there to bring me ecstasy.

In an embrace only lovers know,
Letting our emotions show.
The tender sighs, the words you hear
Expressing my love for you my dear.

TO AWAKEN YOU

I awaken knowing you are near
your quiet breathing I now hear.
Do I dare just reach for you,
knowing you'll awaken if I do.

I long to feel your warmth, and
feel your breath against my skin.
To press my breasts against you,
the way two lovers do.

To gently touch with fingertips,
leaving small kisses with my lips.
To hear you sigh and then awake
to run my hands along your hips.

To kiss your eyelids, in the dark
sliding ever closer as I do.
My love it's nice to awaken you.
Hoping you enjoy that too.

TO LIVE A DREAM

Now that we have lived a dream,
Where will our hearts go?
The part of me I leave with you,
How can I again be whole?

Can we forget the feelings,
Will they fade in time?
Do you share these thoughts,
Or are they only mine?

The sound of you, your laughter,
Places we have been.
How long will you remember the feel,
Of my lips upon your skin?

To just close my eyes and know
You are here, so close to me.
How do I awaken from a dream.
That became reality?

TRUE LOVE

To find a love that is so true,
love that awakens each part of you.
To know real ecstacy beyond the bliss
and feeling the tingling of each kiss.

A love that sets your spirit free
to heavens heights you soar with me.
Your touch ignites my very soul
from just a spark to burning coals.

The embers of a raging fire
your kisses fill me with desire.
To see the sunlight filter through your hair,
or listen to your voice on a breath of air.

Your skin like petals from a rose
and beauty from within that glows.
By moonlight, candlelight, starlight too
my longings love are just for you.

I'm never unclothed for the world to see,
as I'm covered by his love for me.
I hear that rapturous unwritten melody
when my love is here with me.

TRUST

On your shoulder dark hair in disarray,
Green eyes now closed in restful sleep.
Your being here keeps bad dreams away,
Will rest knowing my secrets you will keep
I find such comfort being close to you.
Here with your arms around me,
I feel a special LOVE so true.
Resting now I share my trust and dreams with you.

SKIPPER

So many different kinds of love-
Friendships; relationships, of every kind.
Deep honest feelings from above,
My love is always on my mind.

A closeness that will never end.
It is the keeper of my soul, you see.
I love the rapture and the breeze
While sailing on the open seas…

It lifts my spirits, calms me,
Can forget all worry and strife.
To drift upon the open sea,
My love my passion, my life.

TWILIGHT TIME

As shadows lengthen outside my door,
and evening sun sinks in the west,
visions appear, and voices on a breeze
sounds muffled by the swaying trees.

Shadows dance, and dim the day
soon darkness will be here to stay.
At just that special moment at night,
part dusk, part dark, yet part light.

My mind then wanders for a spell
and of the past my thoughts do dwell.
The visions come, they talk to me!
Oh how great if all could see.

See the shadows from the past
hear the voices of long ago.
How I wish this time could last
voices tell me things I need to know.

A paradox of dark and light
soft gray shadows that come at night,
bringing the voices and visions I see,
like ghostly Spirits watching over me.

TWO YEARS

I sit at my window looking east,
And watch the snowflakes fall.
Was it the same two years ago?
I really cannot recall.

Was lonely then as cold winds blew,
I remember that as I talked to you.
View is much the same, its snowing yet,
I have found warmth I won't forget.

The warmth of your friendly smile,
Glad you were here for a little while.
Your caring changed my snowy view
I now look east and think of you.

I think of all our happy times,
The laughter jokes and fun.
I sit and write my little rhymes,
Sometimes about the things we've done.

I write about my dreams, my fears
Can not believe it's been two years
I'm happy as I watch the snowflakes fall,
But meeting you was best of all.

WHISPERS IN THE DARK

The trees like lace against the sky,
dancing, swaying in the fading light.
Snowflakes flutter and swirl on high.
Darkness will be early here tonight.

The cry of a mountain lion echoes near
he'll feed tonight then disappear.
The hoot of an owl I faintly hear,
This night no stars will appear.

With only the sounds here in the night,
my lovers arms will hold me tight.
He will see me with his fingertips.
I will seek and find his lips.

In velvet darkness that hems us in
just cuddling with the one I love.
No need for any kind of light,
just whispers, here in the night.

TRUE LOVE

To find a love that is so true,
love that awakens each part of you.
To know real ecstasy beyond the bliss
and feeling the tingling of each kiss.

A love that sets your spirit free
to heavens heights you soar with me.
Your touch ignites my very soul
from just a spark to burning coal.

The embers of a raging fire
your kisses fill me with desire.
To see the sunlight filter through your hair,
or listen to your voice on a breath of air.

Your skin like petals from a rose
and beauty from within that glows.
By moonlight, candlelight, starlight too
my longings love are just for you.

I'm never unclothed for the world to see,
as I'm covered by his love for me.
I hear that rapturous unwritten melody
when my love is here with me.

WHEN YOU MAKE LOVE TO ME

Oh how wonderful it will be
When you make love to me!
Our satisfaction will be complete
Once loving seeds are sown.
And I will bask in great content
When both our passions are then spent.

My warmth and wetness there within
As you enter me deep within.
I rise below to match your lust,
And sigh so softly at each thrust.
My breasts rise, like a wave upon the sea.
I hear your voice, as you make love to me.

Our satisfaction we will know as one.
To feel complete, when this is done.
Your commanding desire, I will feel
My broken heart you will heal.
We will both know ecstasy you see,
When you my dear make love to me.

III

Miscellaneous Poems

Most of the following poems were written using nicknames from the 50s Park Chat room.
Or for the people that go there.

MY VALLEY

The piercing cry of a HAWK, breaks the silence of the meadow.
A CHIPMUNK pauses, and listens to the sound.
Tall pines sway and cast an eerie shadow.
Wise OLD OWL is looking all around.
ELK grazes quietly, with lofty antlers high.
Sky is LOST IN BLUE as RAINBOW does appear.
MAMA BEAR with cubs comes strolling by.
Wild geese! or an echo, what did I hear??
Peaceful valley, wild flowers, sun is setting soon.
COYOTE, raccoons, others will come tonight.
All is quiet in my valley in the moonlight.

To my 50s chat room friends

CHAT ROOM CHAT

Wandered in to a chat room one day,
Surely did not plan to stay.
Thought what is going on in here?
TTYL-LUWAMH-((()):**oh dear,
What language do they speak in here?
Some one just said U want to have a QSO with me?
QSO==what is that, did not know the chat U.C.
TTYL-BRB-this makes no sense 2 me.
There are things-*S*-(((echo))) is that obscene?
Some 1-help is this a dream?
Squiggles and giggles, a naked MAN comes in.
AFAIK-BF-ROTFLMAO-that a sin?
Got here this afternoon, now it is dark,
Oh what fun here in this PARK.

TTYL=talk to you later
(((----)))=hug
LUWAMH=love you with all my heart
*(((----))):**=hugs and kisses*
QSO=conversation
BRB=be right back
S=smile
AFAIK=as far as I know
BF=boy friend
ROTFLMAO=rolling on the floor laughing my ass off.

JOHNY ANGEL

Unleashed emotion, or hidden pain
what is there behind your name?
Angel! does bring so much to mind,
is there a paradox here to see??
Angel or Devil, now you tell me!!

KD--4C—SZ--all can hear, few can see,
how many will know the real HE?
Listening to old songs, brings memories
some happy, some sad, yes both of these.
With a nick like Angel, does his mind take flight?

Does he have sweet dreams at night?
Johny Angel, friend from the NET.
Unseen friend I've never met.
Hoping all your dreams come true.

4 ACES

4 Aces from Texas the gamblin man
Just blew into town.
But he's not on the lamb.
4 Aces 4 Aces that high rollin man.

Always a party when this gent's on hand.
Good horses, fast dogs, 21 if you choose,
Lets have a party, what's there to lose?
Lady luck by his side, he surely will win.

Good luck charms welcomed, bring'em on in.
Las Vegas, Tahoe, lets give Reno a try.
Stand back girls this is my kind of guy.
Life is a gamble, for this gamblin man.

Just try and tame him, see if you can.
4 Aces-4 Aces you light up my night.
Luck be not a stranger, keep Aces in mind,
And may his opponent never hold five of a kind.

ANDY

I took his E-Mail from my list,
Deleted his number from ICQ.
No longer is his name upon my screen.
I see him now only in my dreams.
His name is carved in stone, far away.
Yet he is here everyday.

I see him in a marshmallow cloud
As it drifts up in the sky.
I hear his laughter in the breeze
As it sways the tall old pine.

Was glad to call him friend,
Even for a little while.
I remember happy times,
Though his name is not online,
He is here, here in my memory.

PARK FRIENDS

I'm so happy here today,
just *lafin@lovin* time away.
Fluffy clouds just drifting by,
not a teardrop do I cry.

DayStar shining oh so bright,
day slips quietly into night.
LaStar casts a silver light
wise owl glides in silent flight.

Melissa, Jon'Lee, a *Bunny* I see
Katrina a *Joy* to chat with you.
My mind wanders, words flow free,
Here in the 50s..it's fun to be.

Bright *Daisey--Roses* too
Red with crayons here today.
The 50s is a place to play.
((((((((((*HUGS*)))))))))) 4-all of you.

WIZZARD

Wizzard, wizzard sitting on a log
Hard 2-C-U midst the fog.

Wizzard, Wizard, with your hair of white
Please grant me 1 small wish 2night.
R-all the little munchkins there with U-?
Wizzard, wizzard just what is it that U-do?
Granting wishes 4-all that ask
Is tat not quite a task?
Wizzard with 2-Z's grant a wish 4-me.

That would B-so nice U-C.
Wise old Wizzard in the park
Love 2 chat with U-till dark.

GUNSLINGER

Gun belt hanging at your hips,
Soft sweet smile upon your lips.
Eyes that hide a hidden quest,
Silver STAR upon your chest.

Gunslinger-so they all call you,
Keeping peace and order is what you do.
Wear that STAR, wear it proudly.
We need a lot of men like you.

JOKER

All eyes light up when you enter the room,
Never sad tidings,sure never gloom.
Starts telling jokes as soon as he enters,
Some for the gals-some for the fellers.

Is there a sad face behind the laughter?
Joker oh joker-what are you after?
Just filling the room with your idle chatter?
Gee you are funny,so what does it matter?

Jokers needed here,where life is in a whirl,
but sometimes dull.
Having you in the room there's never a lull.
PM Land is fun,you brighten the day.
Keep up the good work,we like it that way.

LOST

White Knight astride your mighty steed,
So glad you came to rescue me.
To you just another good deed,
I really was quite frightened, you see.
In the haunting hours before the dawn,
Wandering alone and lost you found me
Frightened as a timid, lonely fawn.
Oh, on so many things we did agree.
Solitude and incognito, suit me well,
Last night was not the time for me to be alone.
Really glad you came along, it was just swell.
Usually my thoughts are just my own.
They often rattle around in my empty head.
Glad to share some of them with you.
White Knight with shining armor, chivalry is not dead.
I bow to you, a thing I rarely do.
Happy you heard a soft whisper in the night.

BULLRIDER

With rope in hand, hat pulled down,
I walk across familiar ground.
And what before me do I see….
Over a ton of brindle furry.

Sparks like fire in his eyes,
A cool head is needed I realize.
I look at him…..He looks at me,
Sizing each other up you see.

He snorts and shakes his head.
I think of eight seconds soon ahead,
Eight seconds,-------Oh what a ride
On top of turning, twisting hide.

He hits the ground, jars my soul,
Just eight seconds take their toll.
Body hurts, block out the pain,
In eight seconds, on the ground again.

Horns that catch the evening sun
In eight seconds, this ride is done.
My body hurts, I am so sore.
Tomorrow I will ride some more.

With the lure of the next rodeo
Knowing there is only eight seconds to go.
That is where my mind does dwell,
Eight seconds on a ride of hell.

On top a bull,----time stands still
To feel his power, to know his will.
To hear the crowd began to roar.
The sound the cowboy is listening for.

To know you've just ridden well,
For eight seconds so close to hell.
On a bull, that is an eternity,
A bullrider----Ya that's me.

COWPOKE

An ol cow-poke sat gazing,
At the campfire's dying light.
Thinking of fat cattle grazing
Thinking of a bar room fight.
A hot meal, and when he didn't have it's price
Before the tourists found his paradise.

He used to round up cattle,
That had drifted far and wide.
Now he's still astride a saddle,
Teachin' dudes to ride.
They come from North, South, East and West,
To this valley he knows best.

They ask the dumbest questions,
Yet they seem to know it all.
Some things I can not mention
One thing though, they'll all leave this fall.
The dudes with big ideas and fancy motor cars
They want to rough it in million dollar bars.

Will they see the splendor of the quiet?
Or the grandeur of all that thrills his soul
Oh, if there's anything to do they'll try it
Though it's a cinch they'll not reach their goal.
Well it's his job to please, he'll do the best he can.
To take the place of cattle, now there's neon lights
And just as often, still a bar room fight.

The joy of wild wilderness is now lost,
When summer daisies nod their head.
Where the mountains stand with a crown of frost.
The splendor of the silence is now dead.
Dudes and tourists have found this tiny
Place of beauty between the poles.
And they've really cluttered up his home,
In Jackson Hole.

"PEAS"

A can of peas upon a shelf,
69 Cents sign says.
But look here by it's side.
Why I cannot believe my eyes.

Another can-----just the same,
this some kind of a grocery game?
79 Cents here upon this can.
Something here I don't understand.

Same weight--same brand--now I see.
This one reads no salt in me.
Costs a dime to not add salt??
This is hard to figure out.

Why does less just cost more?
Will read the labels--learn some way
to figure just why less is more.
Costs nothing to put nothing in.

I hate to shop now I know why.
Nothing is as meets the eye.
Confusion is my middle name.
I bet both these cans are just the same.

STORM

The black clouds rolled way up high,
As lightning lights the evening sky.
The thunder crashed, the wind did blow,
Bending tree tops, what a show.

Natures great display of lights,
Tis one of my favorite sights.
Summer Storm, dancing in the air
Echoing sounds for all to hear.

Spirits from so far above
Wetting earth with tears of love.
Tears to make the forests grow.
Tears to sprout the seeds we sow.

Tears to wash our pain away,
Ready to start a brand new day.
Storm clouds brewing in the sky,
Without your tears our earth would die.

So rumble, roar; pour forth your love
From the earth below to the sky above.
The Storms of summer do bring me glee
Your tears do show your love for me.

COUNTRY GIRL

A country girl, met a city guy
They met one day just passin by
He won her heart, with one red rose
She won his with words and prose.

Now city guy he sips his wine
A fancy place he likes to dine
Country girl, well she sips tea
And dresses funny, for all to see.

City guy with his knowing ways
Has set country girls heart ablaze,
Oh my gosh he treats her fine
Still she will not sip the wine.

Taking her hand, he'll show the way
For she may move to the city someday.
Country girl on a mountain so high
Oh how she loves her city guy.

HUGS @ KISSES

I am planting a garden of hugs and kisses
Maybe for luck I'll throw in some wishes.
Hoping they grow well, so I may share,
Will then send them to show I care.

I planted the seeds, will watch them grow,
Plan on sending them to all I know.
To start your day will send one to you,
Straight from my garden that I will do.

Hugs and kisses and wishes to start the day,
Knowing these will chase the blues away.
The garden was planted with love you see
To brighten the day for both you and me.

HAND IN HAND

In the early dawn
waves lapping at our feet,
laughing like small children
building castles in the sand.
Walking, talking, hand in hand,
soft breezes like kisses on our skin,
sharing thoughts from deep within.
Taking comfort from each other,
finding contentment, building dreams.
Being together hand in hand,
slowly walking in the sand......

HAPPY TIMES

Darling am I in your thoughts,
Or just a faded memory?
Do you remember our first kiss,
That summer day your lips met mine?
The soft cool rain upon our skin,
Your hand holding mine.
Our laughter in the moonlight,
Oh! What a happy time.
Are these your memories too,
Or are they mine, just mine?

HELL

Stranger", Howdy, you just told me to Go To Hell,"
will tell ya what I'll do,
You show the way, and I will follow you.
It aint a place ya can just go, oh no, oh no.
The Hell I live is here on earth, well so
would gladly go to yours my friend.

Then I could rest a spell, so watch it stranger
when you tell me,"To go to Hell."
I been there,!! Done that, most every day.
You got a problem with me stranger?
I'll live in your Hell any day.
Just come on over, show me the way.

PINK & CRIMSON ROSES

The tangled, twisted wreckage,
That once had been a car.
Now lying midst the roses
Wild roses, from the road not far.

Pink roses, still damp with
Early morning dew.
Some now stained crimson,
By the blood of two.

But what of the third,
Oh, will he be all right?
He's talking, he knows me,
I sat by him all night.

He promised he'd see me tomorrow,
One promise he did not keep.
After I left that morning
He slipped into eternal sleep.

I hadn't told him what I should,
That both our friends were dead.
I only sat and listened, just
Listened to the words he said.

My friends, now gone forever,
I knew not what to do.
So I went out to the roses
And there I said good-bye to you.

"THE DARK"

The darkness held such hidden terror,
far beneath the sun above.
For my own safety I did not care
For the job I did, there was no love.

Small dark tunnels leading every where,
a maze in which I crawl.
Not knowing who was waiting there,
or if the earth above would fall.

I could not hesitate, or even think,
I went to seek, to find, to do.
The unexpected can happen in a blink.
My job is done by such a few.

It's over now, except dreams and memory.
At night it haunts me still, and yet
it's part of me, it had to be.
Would like to close my eyes, and forget.

Forget the smells, the fears, the dark
the blood, from self and adversary.
The job of a tunnel rat is not a lark,
so long ago, yet I am still wary.

Have met a friend, she loves the night.
We talk, we share our so different past.
With her love, I will be alright.
Will find some peace at last.

To her the dark is calm and soft,
soothing, quiet, filled with moonlight.
As gentle as a lovers touch,
knowing she cares now lets me sleep at night.
Again my troubled mind will be alright.

0-595-74906-2

Milton Keynes UK
Ingram Content Group UK Ltd.
UKHW010623050324
438717UK00001B/7/J